ETHIOPIA
THE JOURNEY
BY AMASTARA

For Tamaya who inspired this
and who changed everything.

Proofreading: Jahteecha, MapucheDub

Weblogistic, e-book: Tapedave

Graphic Design: Dubdem

Dub Logistics: Senor Açai, Nads
and many others who are in the shadows

Excerpts from John trudell taken from
interview he did with "Indian Country Today"

PUBLISHED BY TFTT | 2016
ADDIS ABABA {ETHIOPIA},
SOSOLAKAM,
WALKIR VERGANI {BRASIL}

ISBN 978-1-927801-04-8

12
FOREWARD

16
ETHIOPIA: THE JOURNEY

18
AMASTARA YAMASATTAR YAMASTAR

34
RAQAYA YARAQQI YARQUI

42
TAHABBALA YATHEBBAK YATHABBAL

56
YAHAYMAN

86
EPILOGUE

94
PHOTO CREDITS

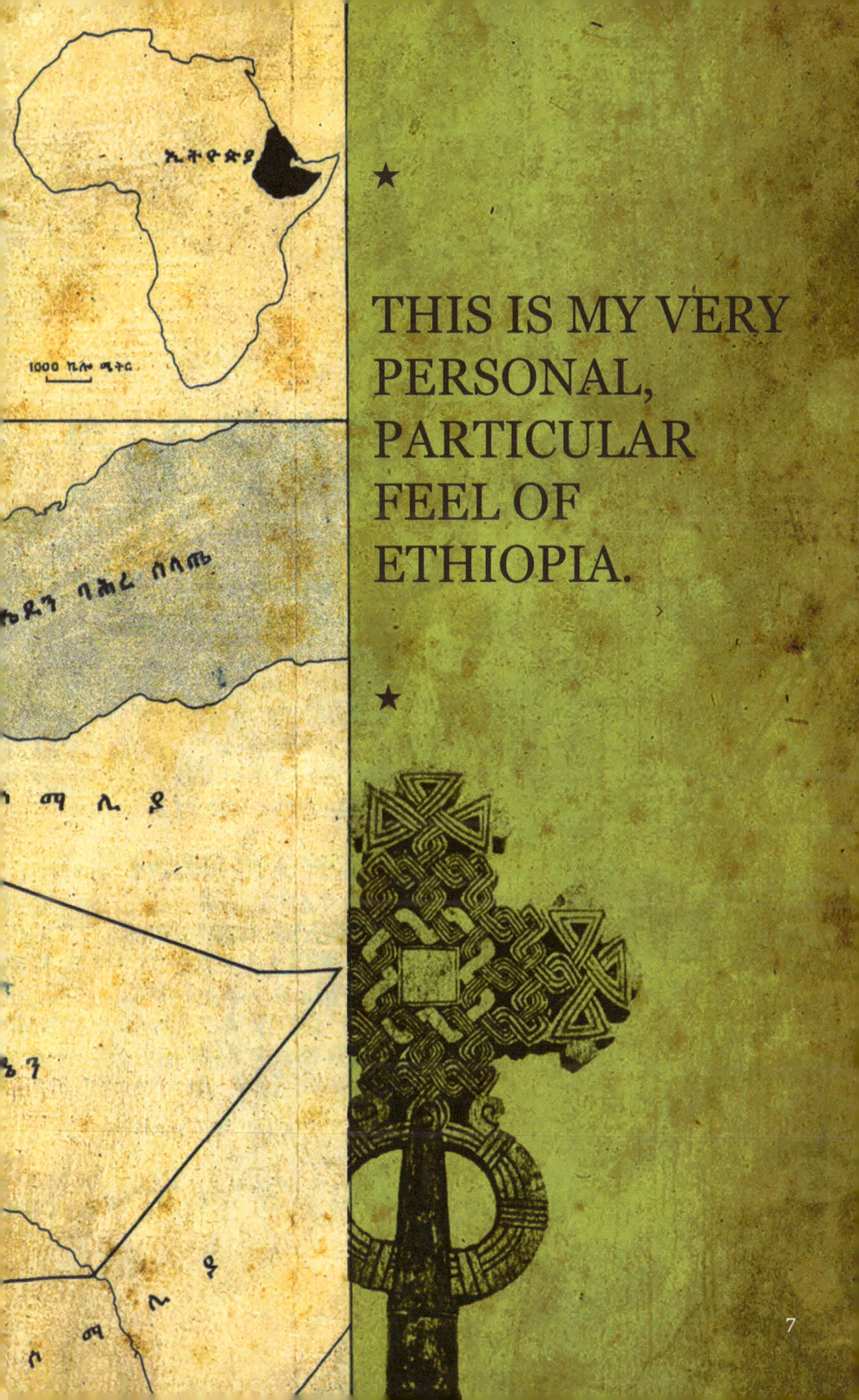

THIS IS MY VERY PERSONAL, PARTICULAR FEEL OF ETHIOPIA.

A spiritual journey

into the dub of Ethiopia

We don't realise
we are human beings.
We need to really look
at who we are.
Its not enough to say
"we are all about respect"
it's not enough anymore,
we have to understand
what we are saying.

John Trudell

ሽ ሃሰተ ሰሰሻሲ ሞሴ ትነ ቀቀሲሻን ቶ ርሲ ሰቁቀሴ
ሮሽ ቢ ቂ ሃዕ ቀ ሽ ቀሴ ሻርሻሴ ቃስቃ
ሽ ሲ ቲ ሰ ሽሰ ሰ ሮ ሰ

neward

FOREWARD

I would like to welcome you to this possibility of embarking on this journey. As I was in the final stage of writing this I had a conversation with an Ethiopian friend Bethel and it addressed and resolved a slight discomfort I had been feeling about publishing this.

I really believe strongly in tolerance and respecting people's choices especially spiritual choices. I don't believe in trying to convert anyone to any form of spiritual belief. If something has its own power then the people will feel it naturally on their own they don't need to be persuaded. That's my personal opinion. It is also your complete right to totally not believe in the spirit world and I experienced some discomfort at the possibility that this writing might be misinterpreted as an attempt to impose that point on view on people. I don't believe in trying to convert anyone to any form of spiritual belief.

I feel it is crucial that people find the strength to be courageous, to find to courage to lead their lives and express themselves in the manner that they themselves desire as opposed to the whims and dictates of others. We need to be courageous!

It really feels to me that we are living in wartime. Even between people, there seems to be a violence, an acridness to the communication. It affects us all.

As I checked into a pension one day I had a conversation with the owner. A simple unassuming man coming from a background of operating grocery stores and welding. He was with a gentle spirit and who spoke like a philosopher poet. He said to me referring to older Ethiopian generations

The people had GRACE back then, you could talk to everyone with no problem... now the people is focussed on this poison called money".

While I'm always a bit wary about nostalgia for the things of the past, I felt he was touching on a much deeper point. I made the connection to thoughts expressed by an Indigenous philosopher from North America John Trudell.

 We don't realise we are human beings. We need to really look at who we are. Its not enough to say "we are all about respect". It's not enough anymore, we have to understand what we are saying. We have to understand tradition, culture, sharing, love. That's the way it was a long time ago. That was our way of life, we looked out for each other. But that's also when as human beings we remembered who we were. Fast foreward to now and there's more carnage from the poverty and racism than there is cohesiveness, we need to use our intelligence clearly and coherently as human beings rather than use our intelligence emotionally as victims. It's all in how we perceive reality".

This book is simply writing which is expressing my perception of my reality.

ETHIOPIA
THE JOURNEY

INTO
THE
MOUNTAINS

Into the mountains I went. I later realized that I had to change buses 6 times to complete my journey. At each stage, some kind person helped me to find the right buses then giving instructions to the driver to make sure I got on the next correct bus. In one instance, I went to pay my fare and was informed that the person who had put me on the bus had already paid for me!

When I finally arrived at the church the whole area was filled with pilgrims. I could see the church perched on the mountain top. Instead of immediately entering I went to the side of the mountain on which the church was perched and which had a view of a forest of eucalyptus trees.

As a sat on one of the many strangely but beautifully shaped boulders, I could see various monks passing by coming from distant areas.

As I sat there I was overwhelmed by the feeling that came over me. It's hard to put into words the feeling that the land in Ethiopia evokes in me. It has such a distinct, unique feel.

Something shimmering, a light feel and at the same time a feeling that one is in a place very profound and multi-layered that you could only just begin to scratch the layers to understand it.

AMASTARA YAMASATTAR YAMASTAR

GEEZ

TO WRITE IN MYSTERIES

Geez is one the most ancient languages of Ethiopia. Two of most widely spoken languages in Ethiopia Amharic & Tigyran originate from Geez. Geez means language of the free! The ancient manuscripts were written in that language and a lot of Ethiopian Orthodox church services are conducted in Geez. I have always been drawn to the language and I'm engaged in trying to learn it. There's just something I love about this language. It was revealed to me that one of the characteristics of Geez is that it words and phrases can have multiple meanings. It is possible to simultaneously express different things with the same words. I was told about the expression "Sem Ena Worq" which refers to the way that something can be expressed so that it has a surface meaning but, in reality, it simultaneously can be expressing something deep and profound and this can be communicated with great subtlety. Essentially it is multidimensional expression. When these characteristics of Geez were explained to me I smiled.

My first thought was "this is a language of code! No wonder I like it!"

Sitting on the mountainside at that moment made me realise something else. Whenever I have been in the mountains in Ethiopia it so often feels that I have lost the weight of my physical being. Barriers are dismantled and its like I can finally begin to see with clarity. This is my very personal, particular feel of Ethiopia.

At one moment, a pair of monks walked by me. A wizened face glanced at me and gave a warm, subtle smile that lit up my heart. I rose and decided to enter the actual church. As I passed through the main entrance I saw that there were two separate lines for different entrances. Uncertain of which one to use I stopped and asked one of the monks who was there.

My question about which was the appropriate entrance lead to an explanation of the protocol involved for entering the church. However immediately our conversation assumed a much deeper tone and suddenly we were in the midst of a very profound conversation about spiritual devotion. This middle-aged man with greying hair explained to me about the devotion of those who devoted themselves to a spiritual life often just drinking a single cup of water per day and a handful of nuts or seeds. As he said to me they don't drink or eat out of immediate desire or need but according to their daily practice and discipline.

These monks and spiritual hermits and mystics (sometimes called Bahtawi) were also known for their commitment to spiritual truth. They had no fear of who they were speaking to whether it be a peasant or a high-ranking political figure. Often these monks or spiritual hermits had dreadlocks.

As I engaged in conversation with this monk I realized something which was for me quite profound. I realized that a couple years ago I had a dream where I was having a conversation with this very same monk and in the conversation he spoke to me about where to go for holy water. So as I spoke to him I asked him if he minded if told him something related to a dream I had. He said sure go ahead. As I related the dream to him he translated to a group of pilgrims who had gathered around listening intently to our conversation. There were people there who had been completely fasting from 3 to 5 days. When I looked into their eyes I was really struck by the strength and determination that emanated from them. I had never witnessed such intensity. I realized I was really in the presence of very serious believers.

When he translated the account of my dream they all looked at me very quietly and some nodded. The monk said to me if you had this dream then you must go to this special place it has the holy water and he gave me directions. He continued to speak to me and I realized he was passing on many spiritual teachings to me with great patience and care.

As I was about to leave his company I asked him if he could please tell me his name.

He said its "Haile Sellassie"

it refers to the Holy Trinity.

When he said this I gasped! I was simply amazed! Different threads were connecting through time and space on this journey in a spectacular way.

I bade him farewell and our conversation was still in my head when I went to join the enormous line for the last transport vehicle back to the town. Standing at the front of the line was a priest with orange robes and dreadlocks down to his shoulders. We smiled at one another.

The previous week I had been to the Holy Trinity church. It had been built by Emperor Haile Selassie. For some months before my journey, I had dreams of visiting this place. Even though I had passed it on different occasions on previous trips to Ethiopia. I had never entered. Something was calling me to this place and I decided to listen.

Once again a kind person on the transport vehicle heard me asking the driver to drop me at the correct location and they offered to show me the right stop. Well, they not only showed me the right stop but they walked with me (out of their way) directly into the churchyard with me, even giving me a mini tour and then excused themselves saying they had to go because they would be late for work. I was really touched by their kindness.

Surrounding the actual church were tombs where people were buried including various notable figures in Ethiopian history. Around that area were places where under the shade of green trees, people were sitting in quiet prayer and meditation. I chose a tree that was tucked a bit back from the church and sat quietly.

As I closed my eyes suddenly I felt like I was being transported to another dimension. I felt like I was hanging in the air. I started seeing beautiful images of people I knew and there was were moments when I seemed to be receiving messages directed to them. When I opened my eyes I was greeted by the sight of the overhanging green branches through which the steeple of the church was visible. I felt the warm sunlight on my skin. It was a moment of exquisite beauty and a sense of beautiful calm.

I decided to leave the church ground without actually entering the church.

Two days later something in my spirit told me to return there.

Having been there before, this time, I found my way easily. I walked around the church grounds which exuded a

beautiful serenity and at that moment, I decided I would actually enter the church. I had to go to the admissions gate and pay for a ticket to go inside the church because it was where they said was the tombs containing the bodies of Empress Menen and Emperor Haile Sellassie.

After purchasing the ticket, I went to the side door of the church. After I took my shoes off a very elderly priest took my ticket and ushered me in. There was a real elegance to the interior of the church but what really caught my attention was the red, green and gold flags that were adorning the ceiling.

The priest came in again and took me to the front of the church where the tombs of Empress Menen and Emperor Haile Selassie were.

I was walking to the back of the church because I wanted to sit and absorb the feeling of the space. However, the priest was very brusquely rushing me out of the church at the same time he very aggressively put out his hand asking for additional money for himself.

It all made me extremely uncomfortable. I hesitated about saying something about it but really I felt that I shouldn't be silencing myself in any way. So I went back to admission office where I bought the ticket and quietly explained that as much as I had been enjoying seeing the inside of the church I felt I had been pushed out by the priest. The admission officer called someone else who I guessed was his boss. Another Ethiopian man arrived and very patiently listened to my story and asked me to please wait. He came back a couple of minutes later with the priest and they talked for quite a while, I got the sense the priest was being quietly reprimanded.

The administrator said to me that he apologized to me for what had happened. He said that the priest had a

MENEN

personal problem and had to rush to the bathroom, that was why I was rushed out. He said to me "I have seen you here before, I have seen you in prayer here before. Please just keep your ticket you can come here anytime to use it. I would also to very humbly invite you to come this afternoon when we have an incense service in the church it would make me very happy if you attend."

The sincerity and courteousness of his offer made me decide to make it a priority for me to return that afternoon. They had made me feel very welcome!

When I returned that afternoon to the church I chose a seat in the front of the church. I didn't realize till the mass started that I was actually sitting in the section where a lot of priests were. A priest entered with an assistant bearing a container with burning incense.

Where I was sitting I had priests on either side of me and also in the front. It was like I was in the middle of a triangle. Suddenly the priests started chanting in Geez. I have always had a high sensitivity to sound.

At that moment, it was like that sensitivity had been enhanced a hundred fold. I was experiencing the singing of the priests as if I was in the middle of a perfect stereo speaker system. I could distinguish sound and frequencies coming from three different directions. Suddenly it was like I was being lifted into the air on a cushion of sound. I could feel myself rising slowly in the church. I was sensitive to all the frequencies from the mouths of the priests. At the same time, the fragrance of the incense wrapped around my senses. I started to see the most beautiful visions. It was like a slow film unfolding in front of my eyes. A film shot with warm luminous light. Tears started to flow. I felt like a layer of dirt had been washed off me. My spirit felt lighter. People that were cut off from me I suddenly was able to communicate directly with them.

My spirit was in another dimension and it was a beautiful feeling.

When I left the church I reflected on a small fact. If I hadn't spoken up about my discomfort and voiced it to the administration I would never have known about or been able to partake in that absolutely amazing experience. I gently but effectively made my voice heard and it was for the better.

 I have learnt from Native people
the most powerful force is soft power,
caring and commitment together.
You need that centre to make
a contribution creatively.
You need its power to make it
realise your vision.
You can have visions and dreaming
but how you realise them depends
on caring and commitment"

Douglas Cardinal

> E LUANA ACOMPANHOU TODAS AS MINHAS VISÕES.

TO SPRINKLE CLEANSE WITH
HOLY WATER

RAQAYA YARAQQI YARQUI

GEEZ

We were climbing in the mountains on very dry giant boulders. In between the rocks, cactus grew. The sky was a brilliant light blue above the dry and arid landscape. I was with a group of friends and one of them a priest who was about to lead us down a secret trail. We were going to a location with holy water. We started descending down into the canyon. It was a very steep climb. Suddenly very unexpectedly in the distance, I noticed the first sign of a stream with a little bit of green vegetation on either side of it. It was in marked contrast to the dry browns of everything around us.

We were directed to climb down another unmarked trail. Now it was like we were walking through a small green jungle as we slipped and slid down the trail making our way through a web of tangled trees and brushes. After quite a while, we reached a flat clearing. It was completely green. A stream with crystal clear icy water ran through the area and there was green grass and tall growing trees with their overhanging leaves. Absolutely everything was a deep green and with the sunlight peeking through it was like we were in an oasis. We were informed that we still had a ways to go. We descended, making our way down very steep slippery hills and through thick flourishing brush.

I wasn't prepared for what I saw after reaching the end of the trail. In front of us was a beautiful cascading waterfall surrounded by the mountain rocks and trees with the water gathering in a pool below. The priest was overjoyed and stripped off all his clothes to bathe under the ice cold water at the same time taking with him containers to collect some of this holy water. To be touched by this water was considered a great blessing.

The rest of us who had never been here being simply astounded. This was a totally hidden place. We would never have imagined that tucked away in these dry arid mountains would be a place so green and lush replete with a waterfall. It reminded me of locations I had been to in the Brazilian Amazon jungle.

Upon reflection, I realized that this was one of the essential things that from my personal experiences which characterized Ethiopia. The best things for me have always been hidden or just under the surface. They have never been obvious or garishly hyped or advertised. Never! It's always been very subtle, What might seem to have very little on the surface is often the exact opposite.

IT'S ALWAYS BEEN VERY SUBTLE, I HAVE ALWAYS HAD TO BE ALERT TO CATCH IT, ALERT TO VERY SUBTLE SIGNS AND INDICATORS.

IT'S ALWAYS BEEN
VERY SUBTLE,
I HAVE ALWAYS
HAD TO BE ALERT
TO CATCH IT,
ALERT TO VERY
SUBTLE SIGNS
AND INDICATORS.

The restaurant only had a small wooden sign with the letters carved on it. In the front of it were a pile of construction material, scaffolding, and a lot of dust. It gave no hint of what really lay inside. As I climbed the stairs I entered a beautifully laid out spacious and extremely elegant restaurant filled with the aroma of delicious food. I was directed up a further set of stairs to where the restaurant owner actually lived.

I was to meet two of my best friends in Ethiopia there, Neway and Asmara.

Nemays' name in Geez means "wealth of spirit" and it was a perfect description of this very kind and super relaxed man. I was introduced to Asmara's friend and owner of the restaurant Tsehai. An Ethiopian woman who had just returned from spending ten days at a retreat for silent meditation. She exuded a very special warmth.

As we enjoyed some of the absolutely mouthwatering food from the restaurant we discussed some aspects of her ten days of silence. We were discussing the importance of silence and quietness, when Asmara made a point which really impacted me. She spoke about how a spiritual teacher of hers had told her that one should only recount an experience 5 times. I was intrigued by this and questioned her more on it. She explained that the thinking was that one doesn't want to become trapped in one's story. That it is important to create a space for new things to happen in one's life and that unfortunately sometimes when people are repeating the same narrative over and over to people it prevents them from moving forward and moving past that.

As someone who has very courageously followed her dreams in life, I always pay close attention to what she says. Later that afternoon Tsehai presented me one of the best moments of my trip. She had spent time helping her daughter

Marly and my friend Asmara get dressed for a gala event that they were going to attend. The two women descended the stairs followed by her. They were breathtakingly resplendent. Truly so. Myself and Neway were making jokes that they were going to be responsible for various earthquakes, tremors and heart palpitations in Addis Ababa.

However as much as my attention was captured by them at that moment I was really observing Tsehai.

When I looked at her face it was filled with pride and joy. Even though at that moment the full attention of the men were on the two other women she was oblivious to this. She was just brimming over with joy. I am very conscious of the fact that we live in the world that encourages women to compete for the attention of men. Yet at this moment, she transcended this pettiness. She didn't anything to try and get any attention. I realized that I was looking at a very self-assured person. Her own inner calm and self-worth shone through at that moment. To me, she literally glowed at that moment and I thought to myself this type of self-assurance and calmness is really something worthwhile to strive to attain.

42

TAHABBALA YATHEBBAK YATHABBAL

TO DARE, TO CHALLENGE SOMEONE

I was walking trying to find an address at night and I was finding it difficult. I stopped to ask a shopkeeper for directions. Standing in front of the shop was a group of youth huddled in the semi-darkness. One of them, head covered with a dirty hoodie asked me if I wanted to buy some weed. I said no. He said "what!? You totally look like you must smoke!" I replied that I don't have anything against herb, but I personally don't need because I can just close my eyes and reach that place of meditation without herb, alcohol or any substance. He smiled and laughed. He liked my answer.

"You mean you can fly like an eagle in your spirit to the place where you want to reach without needing to take anything".

This time, it was my time to smile. I said yes kinda like that. And we both laughed and he gave me a high five.

"I know exactly where that building that you are trying to find is. I can take you". He told me. I said ok let's go. So we started walking on the dark semi-lit streets of Addis Ababa. As we walked, we talked. He had no father and his mother was from Eritrea and was in a refugee camp in another part of the country. He was alone in the city trying to survive on the streets.

As we walked he spoke to me about his life and after a while, he spoke to me about his dream to learn music at a music school. But he said it was impossible he had no money. We started discussing practical possibilities whereby he could get some musical instruction that might not involve money.

In the middle of our conversation, he stopped walking and turned to me said. But this is impossible! No one is going to listen to me! No one is going to pay attention to me.

Normally on the streets when the white people see me they tell me to get away from them. They shoo me away. They just see me as a homeless boy who sells weed and chews chat (chat is a stimulant and mildly narcotic plant).

I said:

"But I'm listening to you!"

"Yes, but you are a spiritual man you are different!"

I just stopped and looked at him. I said:

"You know the only thing I can really do is to talk to you as honestly, truthfully and as directly as possible.

Are you ready for that?"

His eyes looked directly into mine and he nodded and we started talking. To be honest, I can't remember all that I said because it felt more like that things were being transmitted through me.

All I know is that I spoke to him straight from the heart. When our conversation was finished he said "I will go and speak to them and they will listen. if I don't go and try how will I ever know the outcome... I must try!"

Once I went to talk with an indigenous medicine man in North America. After offering him a pouch of tobacco as is the custom, he sang and played his hand drum and offered prayers to the creator.

He spoke to me of visions he saw and messages he received. He said to me you know the people thank me for the advice I'm giving them, but it's not me, I'm just a medium through which this guidance flows. At this moment, I completely realised to the fullness what he meant.

At this moment, I also remembered something he said to me at that moment without me even mentioning the subject.

It was pointed out to me that in the same way indigenous people in North America use sweetgrass for ceremonies that also in Ethiopia sweetgrass is also grown and in the Ethiopian Orthodox church it is burnt and used alongside traditional Ethiopian incense etan.

He said if you want to go to Africa go there.
Follow your heart. You have to put yourself out there!
Two days later I booked my ticket to Ethiopia.

It is through action or non-action
that we allow things to happen,
we must put an end to the idea
of allowing things to happen
and not take responsibility.

Jeannette Armstrong

I think as native people we have
to be very careful about how
we identify ourselves.
I think we need to identify
as human beings and start
thinking like human beings
because whatever is coming,
it's bringing more hard times
for everybody.
We need to look at and
understand responsibility.
We need to understand it
and incorporate it into
our daily living.

John Trudell

TO BE A BELIEVER

A warm light arced across the grounds of the church
believers in traditional white were walking past me
I was bathed in the sunlight
reflecting in the holy feel of the church grounds

so often when I sat here

I felt I was taken
into another dimension

when the priests started chanting
I was lifted higher
on that evening as they reached certain notes
my heart opened up

tears of joy flowed gently down my cheeks
the notes were cleansing
they were a possibility of what we could be

so often when I heard certain singing in Ethiopia
I was reminded of the same frequencies when traditional
indigenous singers in North America sat around the big
drum and chanted.

The frequencies that flowed from their throats in song
would elicit the same emotion in me.

sitting on the church steps, I reflected on
the past month in Ethiopia
so many visions
visions that came to pass
when the spiritual thought becomes a reality

in the mountains, I had climbed for hours up steep rocks
amidst breathtaking views
and never seeing a single tourist
reached a church hardly known
a priest had to be called to unlock it
red green and gold lined one of the pillars of the church
for a moment when I stood there
light surrounded me
I was transported to another place
a vision was shown to me how to help some people

twenty hours later
exactly what I saw in that vision occurred
a force acted through me and I was able to help
a young couple in a mighty wondrous way

in this churchyard
I sat reflecting on my last week in the city
all week my spirit had said to me
keep quiet
keep quiet
be silent
just be quiet and wait
wait for the things to seek you out

even though I had been waiting for this trip for many
many months
and I had a full potential agenda
lists of people to see
I kept quiet
spending more time just walking and sitting around
the church ground
sitting and reflecting in the sunlight
my friends teased me
they asked me if I was becoming a monk
what they said no shuruba
they couldn't believe
but in the silences
that were warmed by sunlight
each day something amazing would happen
**people with spiritual knowledge came to me
and shared with me**

I had walked and talked with a homeless youth
and lifted his spirit opened his eyes to his possibilities
each day someone shared something with me that deeply
affected me, each day im part of something that is heart
warming or thought provoking.

a very young man
young in physical years but with a spiritual wisdom
of an elder
through my intervention and and spiritual support,
for the first time professes his love for a young woman,
in front of her he says

"from the first moment I laid my eyes on her, I loved her.
But I have never tried to control her. I never try and stop
her calling or talking to any boy. I want her to know that
she is free as a bird, but I believe that she loves me and
she will always come to me because she wants to,
not because I have forced her"

She had secretly loved him too but **didn't know**
and had been waiting and **wanting to know**
and now she did.

on another day a wonderful couple invites me to sit
and chat with them we end up talking for hours.
The conversation is very open and poignant.
It just warmed my heart and gave me hope for the future
to see a couple operating with such mutual respect
 for one another

it was espcially inspiring to see a man who realised that
trying to dominate and control a woman was a futile path
instead he chose to display his love for her by respecting
and valuing her freedom

as opposed to do so through jealously and possessiveness
and she did the same for him
showing him the same respect.
our conversation ends back in the church ground
moments of silence bathed by sunlight
more moments of silences
warmed by the sunlight

just walking quietly
quietly

sitting and sometimes just feeling a great spiritual
expanse in front of me

at times it would wrap itself around me
I would feel my palms tingle
light and visions would appear

in the silence and warm sunlight

here I was in the churchyard
my last hours in Ethiopia

and I was sitting alone
just in that day I had turned down four invitations
all with cool, cool women
my friends couldn't believe

you are really training to be a monk they joked
(and I'm sure there are folks out there bewildered
even a bit upset my non communication)

I even passed by without entering musical venues
that I would normally frequent

but my spirit told me
to be quiet just wait

and that afternoon something kept me at the church
in the silence bathed by sunlight
finally I got up to leave
saying my final farewell

as I was walking down the exit

in the most unexpected way
someone approached
I was so surprised
it was like she appeared from another dimension
I didn't see her coming
and I'm a very alert person

but in a few seconds after I heard the sound of voice
**I knew this what was about to unfold
was something very special**

her voice pulled me in
I felt I was transported up the air to one of the giant
green tinged mountains that I had recently visited
and then gently placed to rest in one
of the immense canyons
a place empty, calm, powerful
where it's almost like the spiritual majesty of the
place commands you to speak honestly
to speak from the heart
and that's what we did
as we spoke visions and energy gently swirled around us
her face and persona evoked remembrances and images
familiar comforting inspiring

the image I love the most of Emperor Haile Selassie
was when he was a child
I saw that in her
other compassionate people I respected
I saw that in her

as we spoke
I could feel the energy swirling around us
it was like we were being quietly transported
simultaneously to another dimension
but we were still firmly in that physical dimension
that was attested to by an elderly Ethiopian woman
telling her that her shoulders were bare and that they
were in a church and they should be covered

I love the pride that some Ethiopians,
especially the elderly have in their culture
and traditions.

I offered her my green scarf that I was carrying
to cover her shoulder
which she graciously accepted
and then her cell phone rang

It was an interesting moment
because
I felt we were communicating simultaneously
in two dimensions
our hearts were having a wordless communication
nestled in the silent giant expanse of the blessed
Ethiopian mountains
and at the same time
our feet were firmly planted on the concrete ground
of the churchyard
and this physical world around was attempting
to interrupt us.

**I have learnt over the years
to pay attention to the small details
indigenous people have taught
me that**

When the cell phone rang
she didn't do what 90% of people do
and glance at it to see who was calling and
then most of the time apologizing but then answering it

she just immediately without looking just switched off
as quickly as she could.

It was a detail I really noticed
it spoke to me about the respect she had for
our communication
and a deeper level reflected a will power and
concentration and determination
to keep our communication on
BOTH dimensions flowing

in these social media times
sometimes it feels like certain words
have become devalued
people saying praise and using flattering adjectives
with questionable sincerity

as she handed me back my scarf
as she prepared to leave
she said me
"I'm giving you back and now it's blessed with LOVE"

sound,
sound,
sound has an incredible
power to reveal
I have been blessed with a sensitivity to sound

when she said the word
LOVE

I really noticed!

the word flowed from her mouth
with the clarity and frequency of crystal clear pure spring
water as it flows from the earth
love is such a sacred word
it's a word I venerate

and I'm disturbed when I hear people use
it an insincere way.

but when the word flowed from her lips
it was said with such a natural sincerity
a pureness of sincerity that I hadn't heard for a long time

it made a powerful impact on me
because it was like I was literally listening
to her heartbeat unfiltered
in full beauty

I was filled with the realisation

that this was was a significant moment and meeting
in my life
there was nothing ordinary about this.
This was going to change my life

when she left for her appointment
I reflected and thought
she was a gift from God
it was like I had been rewarded for my belief
it had been the reason why my spirit had been instructed
to wait and be quiet

and despite many things dangled in front of me
I had done that

and in my very last hours in Ethiopia she had appeared
and she touched my heart
even though I didn't want to have the wonderful feeling
I was experiencing jarred by volume of club music
at that moment I felt I had to be brave and follow
my heart

and reaffirm to her how our meeting affected me

as I entered the club jam packed with people
I felt a hand on me
she had spotted me right away
outside

we exchanged words
spoken and unspoken
when I kissed her skin
it had the coolness and texture of being in a lake bathed
only by moonlight

soothing energising powerful
vibrant in an understated powerful way
I was taken to another place
a beautiful place

a doorway opened in my heart
And the light poured in
And it came from her

theres a very powerful Geez word

yahayman

it means
to be a believer

now I'm finally starting to appreciate the full depth
and dimensions of that word.

EPILOGUE

in another city another country another continent

the same scarf she had blessed
had become like a magnet
being specifically responsible for initiating conversations
with some very spiritual people
who approached me asking me about my scarf

I run into an indigenous sistren Maria

and she says to me
**"we keep continuously learning
and learning
its part of the cycle of life
and then we go home....."**

PHOTO CREDITS

Cover: Ethiopian church > Amastara, 2015.

Pag. 2, 3: Ethiopian kingdom.

Pag 6, 7: Ethiopia`s map; traditional cross > from "The Ethiopian Cultiral Heritage", Ministry of Culture of Ethiopia, 1977.

Pag. 8,9: Ethiopian church > Ministry of Culture of Ethiopia, 1977.

Pag. 11: John Trudell > Larry Schreiber – Rpa - Minneapolis Star Tribune, May 23, 1974.

Pag. 14,15: Ethiopia´s flag > Zhax, Shutterstock.

Pag. 16: The mountains > Amastara, 2015.

Pag. 17: Traditional cross > from "The Ethiopian Cultiral Heritage", Ministry of Culture of Ethiopia, 1977.

Pag. 23: Debre Birhan Selassie church, Gondar >milosk50, Shutterstock, March 23, 2014.

Pag. 24, 25: Church in the mountains > Amastara, 2015.

Pag. 26: Priest Asheten Mariam, Lalibela > Hector Conesa, Shutterstock, August 3, 2011.

Pag. 27: Priest holding a candle in the night and reading a book in Geez, Gonder > Fabio Lamanna, Sutterstock.

Pag. 29: Queen Menen.

Pag. 30: King Haile Selassie.

Pag. 33: Church ceiling in Bahar Dar Bahir Dar > JM Travel Photo

Pag. 34, 35: Holy water > Amastara, 2015.

Pag. 38, 39: Holy waterfall > Amastara, 2015.

Pag. 41: The mountains > Amastara, 2015.

Pag. 42, 43: John Trudell speaking > Ilka Hartmann, 1971.

Pag. 46:	North American indigenous ceremonie.
Pag. 47:	Priest > Amastara, 2015.
Pag. 49:	Jeanette Armstrong > Reos Partners, 2015.
Pag. 50:	Ethiopian tribe Dasanech, Omo Rift Valley > demidoff, Shutterstock, November 25, 2011.
Pag. 51:	Mapuche indigenous woman.
Pag. 52:	John Trudell > Clem Albers, 1971.
Pag. 53:	John Trudell > from "Incident at Oglal", Miramax Films / Everett Collection, 1992.
Pag. 55:	John Trudell > English Department and American Indian Studies, University of Idaho Moscow, 2003.
Pag. 56, 57:	Ceremony of the Mursi tribe > Dietmar Temps.
Pag. 58:	Apachita.
Pag. 60, 61:	traditional indigenous singers from Noth America > Student Savy
Pag. 62, 63, 64, 65, 66, 67:	Mystic church > Amastara, 2015.
Pag. 74, 75:	Forest on the way to mountains > Amastara, 2015.
Pag. 76, 77:	The valley > Amastara, 2015
Pag. 79:	Lij Tafari Makonnen {Haile Selassie, age 3}, 1895.
Pag. 85:	Chief Poundmaker {Pitikwahanapiwiyin}, late 1800s.
Pag. 86, 87:	complex of temples in solid rock in Lalibela, Ethiopia > Rafal Cichawa
Pag. 89:	Brazilian Umutima > José Idoyaga/Survival, 1957.
Pag. 90, 91:	John Trudell > Richard Drew, Associated Press, June 14, 1971.
Pag. 92, 93:	Negus warriors.

www.ingramcontent.com/pod-product-compliance
Lightning Source LLC
Chambersburg PA
CBHW041623220426
43662CB00001B/27